SHW

What Happens at a Vet's Office?/
¿Qué pasa en una clínica veterinaria?

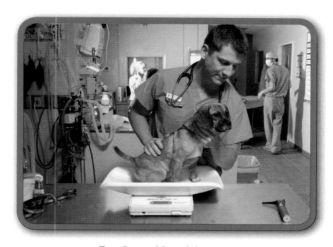

By Amy Hutchings

Reading Consultant: Susan Nations, M.Ed.,
author/literacy coach/consultant in literacy development

WEEKLY READER®
PUBLISHING

For a complete list of Where People Work titles,
please visit our web site at **www.garethstevens.com**.
For a free catalog describing Gareth Stevens Publishing's list of high-quality books,
call 1-800-542-2595 (USA) or 1-800-387-3178 (Canada). Our fax: 877-542-2596

Library of Congress Cataloging-in-Publication Data

Hutchings, Amy.
     [What happens at a vet's office? Spanish & English]
     What happens at a vet's office? / ¿Qué pasa en una clínica veterinaria? / by/por Amy
     Hutchings; reading consultant, Susan Nations.
        p. cm. — (Where people work = ¿Dónde trabaja la gente?)
     Includes bibliographical references and index.
     ISBN-10: 1-4339-0079-3   ISBN-13: 978-1-4339-0079-2 (lib. bdg.)
     ISBN-10: 1-4339-0143-9   ISBN-13: 978-1-4339-0143-0 (softcover)
     1. Veterinarians—Juvenile literature. 2. Veterinary medicine—Vocational guidance—
     Juvenile literature. I. Title. II. Title: ¿Qué pasa en una clínica veterinaria?
  SF756.H8818   2009
  636.089—dc22   2008038542

This edition first published in 2009 by
Weekly Reader® Books
An Imprint of Gareth Stevens Publishing
1 Reader's Digest Road
Pleasantville, NY 10570-7000 USA

Executive Managing Editor: Lisa M. Herrington
Creative Director: Lisa Donovan
Designer: Michelle Castro, Alexandria Davis
Photographer: Richard Hutchings
Publisher: Keith Garton
Translation: Tatiana Acosta and Guillermo Gutiérrez

The publisher thanks Brett Levitzke, DVM, Medical Director of the Veterinary Emergency and
Referral Group in Brooklyn, New York, for his participation in the development of this book.

Printed in the United States of America

1 2 3 4 5 6 7 8 9 10 09 08

Hi, Kids!

I'm Buddy, your Weekly Reader® pal. Have you ever visited a vet's office? I'm here to show and tell what happens at a vet's office. So, come on. Turn the page and read along!

— — — — — — — — —

¡Hola, chicos!

Soy Buddy, su amigo de Weekly Reader®.

¿Han visitado alguna vez una clínica veterinaria? Estoy aquí para contarles lo que pasa en una clínica veterinaria. Así que vengan conmigo. ¡Pasen la página y vamos a leer!

Boldface words appear in the glossary.

— — — — — — — —

Las palabras en **negrita** aparecen en el glosario.

Animals go to the doctor, just as you do. A **vet** is a doctor who cares for animals. Jane's dog, Ginger, goes to the vet for a **checkup**.

— — — — — — — — —

Los animales también van al médico. El médico que atiende a los animales se llama **veterinario**. Jane lleva a su perra Ginger al veterinario para que le hagan un **chequeo**.

First, a worker signs the family in at the desk. She takes their name and keeps track of Ginger's records.

– – – – – – – – – –

Primero, una trabajadora en el mostrador anota a la familia. Apunta sus nombres y busca el historial de Ginger.

Then they sit in the waiting room. The waiting room is filled with owners and their pets.

— — — — — — — — — —

Después, Jane y su madre se sientan en la sala de espera. Allí hay muchas personas con sus mascotas.

9

Now it is Ginger's turn! The vet's helper, called a **vet tech**, weighs Ginger on a **scale**.

— — — — — — — — — —

¡Ahora le toca a Ginger! La asistente del veterinario, o **auxiliar de veterinaria**, pesa a Ginger en una **báscula**.

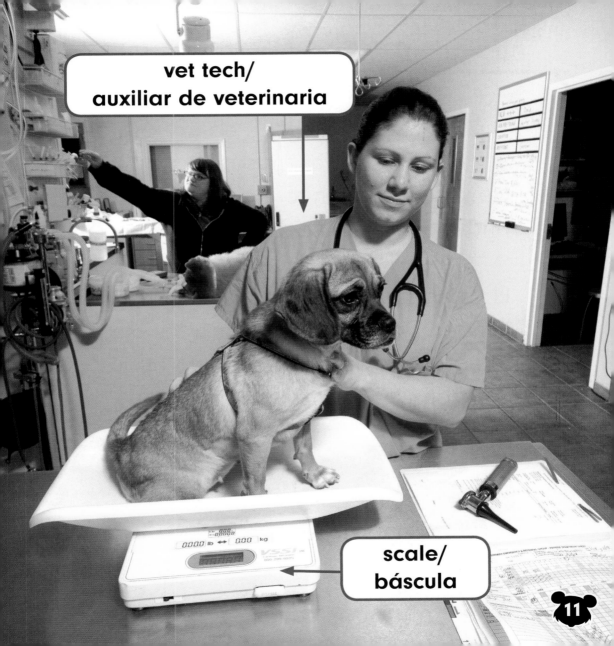

The vet checks Ginger's ears. Next, he will check her eyes, nose, and mouth. He will also listen to the dog's heart and feel her stomach.

— — — — — — — — —

El veterinario le revisa los oídos a Ginger. Después, le revisará los ojos, la nariz y la boca. También le oirá el corazón y le tocará la panza.

vet/
veterinario

13

Ginger is a good **patient**. She gets a **shot** to keep her healthy.

– – – – – – – – –

Ginger es una **paciente** muy buena. Le ponen una **inyección** para que no se enferme.

shot/
inyección

15

The vet learns that Ginger stepped on a thorn. He checks the dog's paw.

– – – – – – – – –

El veterinario nota que Ginger pisó una espina y le examina la pata.

Ginger gets an **X-ray** taken of her paw. A lab worker looks over the X-ray. Good news! Ginger's paw is fine.

– – – – – – – – – –

Después, toman una **radiografía** de la pata de Ginger. Una técnico de laboratorio revisa la radiografía. ¡Buenas noticias! La pata de Ginger está bien.

X-ray/
radiografía

19

Ginger is healthy. The vet tells Jane how to care for Ginger. Jane gives Ginger a big hug!

— — — — — — — — —

Ginger está sana. El veterinario le explica a Jane cómo cuidarla. ¡Jane le da un gran abrazo a su perra!

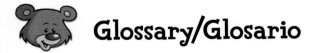

Glossary/Glosario

checkup: a medical exam to make sure a person or an animal is healthy

patient: a person or an animal who goes to the doctor or vet

scale: a machine that weighs things

shot: an injection of medicine

vet: an animal doctor (short for *veterinarian*)

vet tech: a trained worker who helps the vet

X-ray: a picture taken with a special camera used to see inside a body

— — — — — — — — —

auxiliar de veterinaria: trabajador preparado para ayudar al veterinario

báscula: máquina que se usa para pesar

chequeo: examen médico que se hace para verificar que una persona o un animal no estén enfermos

inyección: medicina inyectada

paciente: persona que va al médico, o animal que va al veterinario

radiografía: fotografía tomada con una cámara especial que permite mirar el cuerpo por dentro

veterinario: médico de animales

For More Information/Más información

Books/Libros
Caring for Your Pets: A Book About Veterinarians.
Ann Owen (Coughlan Publishing, 2003)

Veterinarian/El veterinario. People in My Community/
La gente de mi comunidad (series). JoAnn Early Macken
(Gareth Stevens, 2003)

Web Sites/Páginas web
American Veterinary Medical Association (AVMA) /
Asociación Estadounidense de Veterinarios (AVMA)
www.avma.org/careforanimals/animatedjourneys/animatedfl.asp
Learn about pets and the people who care for them./
Aprendan cosas sobre las mascotas y las personas que las cuidan.

Petpourri from the AVMA/Petpourri de la AVMA
www.avma.org/careforanimals/kidscorner
Find fun activities to learn how to care for pets./Encuentren divertidas
actividades para aprender los cuidados que requiere una mascota.

 # Index/Índice

About the Author

Amy Hutchings was part of the original production staff of *Sesame Street* for the first ten years of the show's history. She then went on to work with her husband, Richard, producing thousands of photographs for children's publishers. She has written several books, including *Firehouse Dog* and *Picking Apples and Pumpkins*. She lives in Rhinebeck, New York, along with many deer, squirrels, and wild turkeys.

Información sobre la autora

Amy Hutchings formó parte del grupo de producción original de la serie *Plaza Sésamo* durante los primeros diez años del programa. Más adelante, pasó a trabajar con su esposo, Richard, en la producción de miles de fotografías para editoriales de libros infantiles. Amy ha escrito muchos libros, incluyendo *Firehouse Dog* y *Picking Apples and Pumpkins*. Vive en Rhinebeck, Nueva York, junto con muchos venados, ardillas y pavos salvajes.